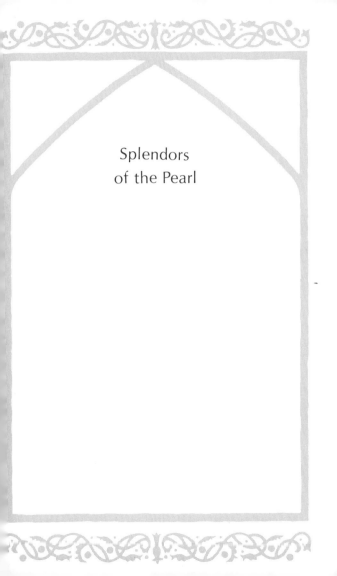

Splendors
of the Pearl

Splendors of the Pearl

The Wisdom of India in Selected Writings

Edited by Robert Wood

Hallmark Editions

Splendors
of the Pearl

$\mathcal{A}$s two pieces of wood
floating on the ocean
come together
at one time
and are again separated,
even such is the union
of living creatures
in this world.

The Mahabharata

*I*n that family
where the husband
is pleased with his wife,
and the wife
with her husband,
happiness
will assuredly
be lasting.

The Laws of Manu

Even the severed branch
grows again,
and the
sunken moon returns:
wise men
who ponder this
are not troubled
in adversity.

Bhartrhari

*G*od respects me
when I work,
but he loves me
when I sing.

Rabindranath Tagore

*I*f a man
speaks or acts
with a pure thought,
happiness follows him
like a shadow
that never
leaves him.

Buddhism

*H*e whose days pass
without imparting
and enjoying
is like
the bellows of a smith:
he breathes indeed,
but he does not live.

from The Hitopadesa

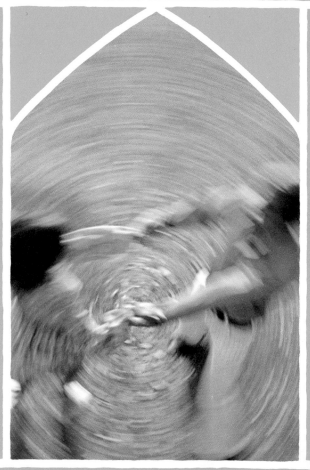

*W*hile life is yours,
live joyously;
None can escape
Death's searching eye:
When once
this frame of ours
they burn,
How shall it
e'er again return?

Carvaka

Sorrow
comes after joy,
and joy
after sorrow.
The joys and sorrows
of human beings
are revolving
on a wheel…

…After happiness,
sorrow has come to thee.
Thou shalt
again have happiness.
No one
suffers sorrow forever,
and no one
enjoys happiness forever.

The Mahabharata

*W*hat we have done
will not be lost
to all eternity.
Everything ripens
at its time
and becomes fruit
at its hour.

Divyavadana

A stone in the shoe,
a gadfly in the ear,
a mote in the eye,
a thorn in the foot,
and a quarrel in the family,
however small in themselves,
are unspeakably tormenting.

from *The Vemana*

*T*he tree of the world
hath its poisons,
but beareth two fruits
of exquisite flavor,
the nectar of poetry
and the society
of noble men.

from The Hitopadesa

*W*hat man is there
whom contact
with a great soul
will not exalt?
A drop of water
upon the petal
of a lotus
glistens with the
splendors of the pearl.

from The Panchatantra

*N*ot even
a dexterous person
can ride
on his own shoulders.

Sayana

God will not ask a man
of what race he is —
he will ask
what he has done.

from The Adi-Granth

*I*f I make
the seven oceans ink,
if I make
the trees my pen,
if I make
the earth my paper,
the glory of God
cannot be written.

The Kabir

*O*ne should give
with faith.
One should give
with plenty.
One should give
with modesty.
One should give
with fear.
One should give
with sympathy.

Taittiriya

*T*his same thing
does the divine voice,
thunder, repeat:
Da! Da! Da!
That is, restrain
yourselves,
give, be compassionate.
One should practice
this same triad:
self-restraint, giving,
compassion.

Brhadaranyaka Upanishad

A defect
will more quickly
take the eye
than a merit.
The spots on the moon
usually
arrest our attention
more than
its clear brilliance.

from The Drishtanta Sataka

*H*idden deep
in the heart of things,
Thou carest
for growth and life:
the seed becomes a shoot,
the bud a blossom,
the flower becomes fruit…

...Tired
I slept on my idle bed
in the illusion
that the work had an end.
In the morning
I awoke to find
that my garden
was full of flowers.

Rabindranath Tagore

A spirit
filled with truth
must needs direct
its actions
to the final goal.

Mahatma Gandhi

*A*s a solid rock
is not shaken
by the wind,
so wise men
are not moved
amidst blame and praise.

Buddhism

*T*hat man alone
is wise
Who keeps mastery
of himself!

The Bhagavad Gita

*T*he union of numbers,
though
ever so little strength
in themselves separately,
makes power;
from leaves of grass,
they twist the rope
that binds
even the elephant.

from The Panchatantra

*T*hink not lightly
of evil saying that
"it will not come near me."
Even a water pot
is filled by
the falling of drops of water.
A fool becomes
full of evil
even if he gathers it
little by little.

Buddhism

Single is each being born;
single it dies;
single it enjoys
the reward of its virtue;
single it suffers
the punishment of its sin.

The Laws of Manu

$\mathcal{A}$s the light goes out
with the exhaustion
of the oil,
so fortune fails
with the cessation
of human endeavor.

The Mahabharata

A wound
made by the arrow
will heal;
a forest
felled by the axe
will spring again
in new growth;
but a wound
made by the tongue
will never heal.

The Mahabharata

*R*iches in their acquisition
bring pain and suffering;
in their loss,
manifold trouble and sorrow;
in their possession
a wild intoxication.
How can we say
they confer happiness?

from The Hitopadesa

Learn true joy
And
you will meet
God.

Sri Aurobindo

This book was set in Optima,
a sans serif face with classic proportions
designed by Hermann Zapf in 1958
for the Stempel Foundry.
Names and credit lines set in Legend,
a distinctive script
designed by F. H. E. Schneidler in 1937
for the Bauer Foundry.
Printed on Hallmark Crown-Pearl paper.